A DIRT ROAD HANGS FROM THE SKY

POEMS BY
CLAUDIA SEREA

8TH HOUSE PUBLISHING
www.8thHousePublishing.com

8th House Publishing
Montreal, Canada

Copyright © 2013 Claudia Serea
First Edition

Cover Design © 2013 8th House Publishing

Set in *Caslon* and *BlackBoris*

A CIP catalogue record for this book is available from
LIBRARY AND ARCHIVES CANADA
CATALOGUING IN PUBLICATION
A Dirt Road Hangs from the Sky / Serea, Claudia (1969-)

ISBN 978-1-926716-24-4

8th House Publishing
Montreal, Canada

*To my grandparents, my parents,
and all the other victims of Communist
repression.*

Contents

A DIRT ROAD HANGS FROM THE SKY

When justice can't serve as a form of memory,
memory alone can serve as a form of justice.

—*Ana Blandiana*

PART I

For the forty soldiers of the XII Legion Fulminata

Sift the flour three times,
for fear, forgiveness, faith.

Make a nest in the middle
and pour the milk.

Think of the frozen Lake Sevasta
embracing the martyrs.

Let yeast foam
and bloom a warm flower.

Break the eggs.

Think of ankles and kneecaps
broken by hammers.

Add lemon zest rinds,
glowing crowns of saints.

Melt butter.
Think of ice melting on soldiers' skin.

Mix with oil and knead
until the dough speaks and breathes.

Breathe.

Pound and throw the dough 100 times.
Torture it.
Tell it to renounce God.

Taste.

Add sugar,
pinch of salt, of patience.

Leave it by the oven to rise, alive.

Make figure eights
shaped like humans,
with heads and bellies
of braided dough.

Brush with beaten egg.

Align the small army.
The forty soldiers of the XII Legion Fulminata
go straight into fire.

Sink them in honey,
sprinkle with chopped walnuts.

Think of the forgotten ones,
known or unknown.

Think of the unidentified,
missing, vanished.

Call out unspoken names.

For them, break apart the *macinici* cake.
Take a bite of its soft body,
fragrant and sweet.

Ask for forgiveness of the wandering,
fugitives, lonely,

ones that lived before us
and are gone.

The first 80,000 are hard; the next 2 million are easy.

1.
Forgive me, Grandma, for not speaking sooner:
my mouth was stitched by my mother and father
who thought it was best that way.

2.
I won't give you anything I won't give you any-
thing I won't give you anything I won't give you
anything I won't give you anything I won't give
you anything I won't give you anything I won't
give you anything. I won't give you any damn thing,

unless you leave me for dead,
and they did.

3.
Cranking up the machine,
the president explains:
The first 80,000 are hard.
The next 2 million are easy.

4.
Send in the troops. Send in the troops.
Send in the troops the tanks the trains
send in the military tribunals the prosecutors the judges
send in the troops the troops the troops
to shoot them chain them jail them send them
where the mute had weaned the mare.

They must be guilty of something:
send in the troops.

5.
What makes a nation bite its own flesh?
How does a country turn cannibal?

In a burlap sack stitched shut,
Grandma abandoned the cat
that ate her own kittens.

6.
Rows, rows, rows, rows.
Rows, rows, rows, rows.

I see my grandfather in one of these rows.
Behind him, his cousins, his neighbors, his
friends.

My father is further away,
in the rows of the young ones, worked to death.

Forgive him, Grandma, for not speaking sooner:
his mouth was stitched with fear.

7.
I am a product of this machine
that feeds on grandparents, on parents,

and spits out the new generations,
memory cards erased,

then swallows us again
and again.

8.
I was there,
in one of the school rows,

my red pioneer tie flapping,
proudly reciting my achievements.

Today, my father lives closer to death
than to his youth in the gulag.

In the grapevine shadow, we visit the past
with flashlights of plum brandy,

and we unstitch it thread by thread,
we tear it apart.

Words around my neck

Tell me, grandma, everything you know,
so I can be your mouth when you're gone.

I'll be one with you.
Your brown eyes will be mine,

your hair, your nails, your breath,
all mine.

I'll wear your words around my neck
on a silver chain with a filigree heart.

I'll keep the necklace
on the table next to me at night,

next to the stained mirror
that has seen it all.

The chain will give a faint glint
and start speaking

when the moon will muster
enough courage to stand witness.

Milk brothers

You were as long as a child's arm
the day I came from the field

and found you between my toddlers
slurping milk from the same bowl,

you, the smallest saint snake
who ticked at night in the wall.

I stared at you,
cold limbs, cold tongue.

A terrible sin to kill you,
but I must do something, I thought,

and the boys turned their heads
and smiled, unafraid,

waived their spoons, splashed milk,
made a mess on the floor.

I could swear you were smiling, too,
as you slithered away.

The time when God lived in the river

After the war, famine married fear
and had many children who spoke Russian,

but God was still swimming, a sturgeon
on the bottom of the river.

That year, the Danube had come huge
and flooded the entire valley.

It left behind Biblical gifts:
tons of fish swarmed the ponds and streams.

People piled the fish in oxen-pulled wagons:
Fish! Fish for sale!

Kids screamed, women hurried,
aprons loaded with live knives.

Fried in corn crust, grilled, stewed, brined,
my grandma cooked fish every day
a different way.

From the kitchen, she'd look down the road
through the yellow pillars of dust

as my father climbed home
counting his catch.

Under the table next to the door

Stepped on by many feet,
we were the specks of dirt on the floor.

We were the crumbs
waiting to be swept

or pecked into oblivion
by a chicken.

We dreamed of escaping,
of running away,

or being carried by ants to their colony,
but we didn't own a passport.

We were the small grapes in a basket
under the table next to the door,

waiting to be crushed by boots,
left to ferment, strained, poured

into a cup and swallowed
by a century already drunk.

PART II

The Dictionary

O

obedient   obey   obituary
object   objectify   obligatory
obliterate   oblivion

O forms in the mouth,
in the throat, above the tongue:

an outward movement of air,
a hollow, round sound.

Open the page at letter O.
See what you find.

> Oancea, Gheorghe. Peasant. Sentenced to
> 15 years.

> Oancea, Ion. Peasant. Arrested with
> his son Stefan, teacher. Tortured by
> Securitate. Sentenced to 10 years and
> his son to 5 years. Wife Agmira and the
> other 2 children deported for 6 years to
> forced labor camps (stone quarries).

> Oancea, Soare. From Bessarabia. Arrested
> by NKVD and deported to Siberia in
> 1946.
> No further information avail.

Oancea, Traian I. Student at the Polytechnic
Institute. Sentenced to 8 years for conspiracy
against social order.

Oancea, Vasile. Tortured by Securitate.
Sentenced to 5 years. Wife Floarea and 2
children deported.

Oancea, Zosima. Priest. Married, father of
4 minors. Arrested because he helped the
families of political prisoners. Sentenced to 9
years.

Name:
A succession of sounds
to which a face is attached.

The name might as well be spelled
by vowels, clangs of shackles,
consonants, thuds
of fists against skin,
bangs of prison doors, rattle
of cattle trains.

*observe   obsessed   obsolete
obstacle   obstinate   occupied   occur
ocean   oculus   ocular*

Ocular. Eye. Eyewitness.

Obancea, Gheorghe. Arrested for
giving food to partisans. Tortured
by Securitate. Sentenced to 15 years
forced labor.

Obarseanu, Florea I. Peasant. Arrested
on October 21, 1959, for activities
against land nationalization. Tortured
by Securitate. Sentenced to 5 years.

Oberding, Dominic. Arrested by
NKVD and sent to forced labor camps
in Siberia.

Oberkirch, Barbara. Born in 1934.
Arrested by NKVD and sent to forced
labor camps in Siberia, where she
died.

Oberkirch, Magdalena. Deported
since 1951.

Obician, Arcadia, Dragutin, Dusan,
Mara. Peasants. Deported on June 18,
1951.

odious   offend   offensive
official   often   old   omen
ominous   omission   only   one

Only one. The one.
Every one is *the* one.
The only one.

They once had bodies,
flesh, voice, life.

Now all that remains
are lists of names,
bones in a cemetery online.

> Olaru, Aurelia. Born on August 19, 1941.
> Arrested on May 5, 1952, 11 years old.
> Deported.

> Olaru, Constantin. Born in 1929. From
> Bessarabia. Deported to Siberia (Kurgan)
> with his wife Alexandra on July 6, 1949.

> Olaru, Constantin I. Worker. Arrested with
> his father Ion and brother Stefan in 1949.
> His cooperation with the investigators
> resulted in multiple arrests.

> Olaru, Petre. Arrested because of
> statements made by his son. Interrogated
> by Securitate, where he was beaten by his
> own son.

ongoing   onslaught   on purpose
open   operate   operative
oppose   opposition   oppressive

Faces blurred,
eaten by time.

A Dirt Road Hangs from the Sky

O forms in the mouth
that blows binary dust across
the computer screen,
byte by byte.

Names, names,
enough to populate a small country
of pain.

But do you hear them scream?

> Oprescu, Gheorghe I. Born on October 28,
> 1934. Sentenced to 5 years
> for conspiracy against social order, then
> deported.

> Oprescu, Grigore S. Sentenced to 2 years
> forced labor.

> Oprescu, Puiu. Economist. Sentenced to 7
> years.

> Oprescu, Toma. Priest. Sentenced to 8 years.

> Opret, Iacob. Peasant. Arrested in
> December 1956. Tortured during
> interrogation. Sentenced to 7 years forced
> labor.

> Opris, Constantin. Lawyer. Sentenced to 5
> years in 1950. Arrested again in 1958 and
> sentenced to 24 years forced labor.

opprobrium   opprobrious   ordain   ordeal
order   orderly   orphan   ostracize   our

Our. Our Father,
Who art in heaven,
Holy is Thy Name.

My father
and his father and brothers.

Our. Our fathers.
Our grandfathers, uncles, brothers.
Their names.

> Opris, Ilie. Greek-Catholic priest.
> Killed during interrogation.
>
> Opris, Nicolae. Arrested because he
> helped several people cross the border
> to Yugoslavia. Sentenced to 12 years.
>
> Oprisan, Constantin Costache.
> Sentenced to forced labor for life.
>
> Oprita, Ileana. Born on January 1,
> 1951. Arrested in 1958 (7 years old)
> and deported.
>
> Oprita, Octavian. College student
> and partisan. Killed by Securitate in
> Apuseni Mountains.

Oproiu, Ion. Arrested with his
father (priest, 74 years old) for
refusing nationalization. Sentenced
to 20 years forced labor.

O forms in my mouth
and in my bones.

O forms in the way my hair follows
the oval of my face,
my father's forehead,
my grandfather's nose.

My blood carries Os.

Search: trialofcomunism.com/
testimonials/
arrested, tortured, imprisoned, killed/
dictionary/N-O/

Scroll down to Orasel,
my maiden name.
It means small town.

Orasel, Eliodor V. Born in 1939. Sentenced to
8 years for conspiracy against social order.

Orasel, Lucian V. Born in 1937.
Sentenced in 1956 to 10 years.

Orasel, Petre Ghe. Sentenced to 6 years
for conspiracy against social order.

Orasel, Vasile. Father of Eliodor, Lucian,
and Petre. Sentenced to 25 years for
refusing nationalization of the land.

Oust   out   outcast   outlaw   outwear
over   overflow   overkill   overwhelm

O, the sound of wind
winding through the hollow of bones.

Chain links, chained Os.
Eyes. The round eyes,
the fixated pupils of death.

Orban, Andrei. Butcher. Killed during
detention, in 1951.

Orban, Carol. Accountant. Sentenced
to death and executed on September 1,
1958.

Orban, Cornel. Sentenced to death in
1956. Executed on September 1, 1958.

Orban, Stefan. Sentenced to death in
1956. Executed on September 1, 1958.

Ordeanu, Danila. Worker. Arrested in
1951. Killed in the Cernavoda camp,
on February 9, 1953.

Orendi, Ioan I. Clerk. Arrested in
1950. Killed during detention in 1952.

Who stole their years,
their lives? Who?

Letters ignite into funeral fires.

The dead are baking ovals of bread.

My grandmother places
torn pieces of meat
into the gaping O
of the pot on the stove.

Oh, the stories untold.

Orescu, Gheorghe V. From Bessarabia.
Deported in camps from Irkutsk,
Siberia, with wife Maia and children
Fiodor, Varvara, and Ecaterina.

Orezeanu, I. County clerk. Arrested
by NKVD and deported to forced
labor camps in Pecioara, Komi region,
Siberia.

Organ, Alexandra E. From Bessarabia.
Peasant. Deported to camps from Cita
region with children Vasilisa and
Victor.

Organ, Ivan I. From Bessarabia.
Peasant. Deported to camps from Cita
region with wife Feodosia and children
Alexandru and Alexei.

Organ, Vasile. From Bessarabia. Peasant.
Deported to camps from Kurgan region
with wife Eudochia and son Andrei.

Overrun   overswarm   overthrow
overturn   own   own up

My own drops,
small drops
in an ocean of Os.

I owe them words,
own,   own up.

Own up to the Os.

PART III

Keep in a safe place the memory of your suffering:
it's the treasure for which you paid the most.
—*Nicolae Iorga*

1958

It was the Year of the Earth Dog
who battled the water metal snakes,
fire wood rats, earth fire rabbits,
wood monkeys, water sheep, fire dragons.

It was the year my father finished high school,
the last year he slept in the freezing attic
where the *crivat* howled,
the last time to put up with Tanti Sita
who'd lock the stove and yell,
Boy, if you're cold, wear another coat!

It was the year Explorer 1 was launched
and Sputnik fell from orbit,
the year Khrushchev ascended to power,
the Red Army left Romania,
Castro took Havana,
unemployment in Detroit was 20%;
the year The King became private #53310761
and Charles, Prince of Wales;
Lolita was published,
instant noodles invented,
NASA established.

It was the year my father wrote
Gone are the coffee, oil, and flour,
The wheat is nowhere to be seen,
Poor, dear Romanian country,
The Soviet People set you free!
and read it to his roommate and best friend.

It was the year of the dog
when grandpa told the Communists
If you wanna take my land,
you'll have to get me first,
then ran away and lived for months
in the cornfields but was caught
when someone coughed up his hiding spot.

It was the year the secret police
ransacked the house and found the poem,
the year my grandma wished she wasn't born,
the year the men were tried by military tribunals
as *enemies of the people.*

The earth dog drank his mother's tears.

Death! Death! Death!
clamored the courtroom audience
of water metal snakes fire wood rats
earth fire rabbits wood monkeys water sheep.

It was the year my father turned eighteen:
a gate opened in the fire dragon's breath
and closed behind him.

It was the Year of the Earth Dog,
the year of the Hammer and Sickle,
of the Fist and Boot,
of Rope and Noose.

Limbo

Shaved head, pale,
eyes not afraid
of God,
or animals,
Taica walked in,
shuffling
his shackled feet,
into the small room
lit by a single bulb.

He looked at the table
and chair, looked
at the cement floor,
washed fresh
by another prisoner,

looked at the two
interrogators
and wondered
how low
would *they* go?

How low
would *he* go?

The things my father has seen

Don't ask me questions, kiddo, my father says.
I've seen people die for nothing,
for yes, or no.

I've seen my own father walk in chains
through the wreckage of an era,
eating death with a twisted spoon.

I've seen the living human remains
wearing angel wings and dirt,
eyesight slurped by leptospirosis.

I've shaved swamps, cut mountains of stalks,
slashed my skin on reeds,
my legs devoured by leeches.

I've lived with the worms
inside the earth's bowels.
For years I carried the clay kiss on my lips.

I've seen the Danube in rags,
a gray monster on my chest,
rising, pulling, grabbing.

I've seen heads covered by water.
I've seen a wall of people fall,
bodies used as live sandbags.

Don't ask me questions, dear,
about the years I stood in hell,
and how I held my friend's hand
until he pulled away.

My father's quiet friends in prison, 1958-1962

Craiova, Gherla, Giurgiu—political prisons
Salcia, Periprava—forced labor camps for political detainees

The gruel

I'm lumpy, lukewarm, and gray,
and you could use me for glue,
mortar, or clay.

Inside your cupped hands,
I breathe my steam,
soft as a prayer.

Dip your tin spoon
inside me.

Lift me
to your hungry lips.

You don't have to like me.

The blanket

I can't protect you from nightmares,
or from the hands that grab you in the dark
and push you back
into the beating room.

Forgive me.

I'm so thin,
worn to threads by the bodies
I covered before you,

I can't even protect you
from the cold.

But I can offer you my checkered field
where you can move the armies
made of bread,

molded with saliva
and hardened
into soldiers,
horses, bishops, towers,
and queens.

At last, this battle is yours to win.

The piece of glass

You guard me with your life.

You spit on me
and smear me
with shavings of soap,

and sprinkle lime dust
from the walls

until I have a new,
smooth skin.

Now I've become a surface
for poems

and equations
with multiple unknowns.

Today's lesson is French,
taught in whispers.

Write down the words
with a sharp twig
and repeat them.

No one can wipe them
off your mind:

Je suis,
tu es,
il est.

I am.
You are.
He is.

We are.

The small stone

All you need
is a stumble

even if you earn
a boot
in the ribs.

And you pick me up,
hide me
under your tongue,
and carry me inside.

I'm your phone,
your postcard,
your smoke signal,

the only one who can talk
through ceilings and walls

and send a coded message
to the man released today:

Ring the bell
to my mother's house

and tell her
I'm alive.

The moon

I come to look at you at night
to see if you're still
curled on your cot.

Thousands of years,
I witnessed
the butchering of men
called history.

I can't help anyone.

I rise,
stir the howls in wolves,
and swell the tides,

but I can't pull you out
from your brother's
murderous arms.

I can only hold
your hope
coins

in a tin cup
in the sky.

Dumitru

If I could pick up your name from the floor,
put it back under my tongue,
swallow it,

I would.

I didn't mean to spit it out
with the vomit and blood
when the blows hit my stomach.

Fragile, a small egg
next to the guard's boot,

your so-called *co-conspirator*
against the social order name

quivers in its placenta
of guilt and saliva

and the hits don't stop,
and shame sears.

If I could take it back,
I would.

Your name.
Given.

Your life.
Taken.

Du-
mitru.

One more day

To Elisabeta Rizea, 1912–October 6, 2003, who was tortured and sentenced to 25 years in prison for supporting the fighters against the Communist regime.

After the beating, comes the rain
and licks my chest with a hundred dog tongues.

I wear a shirt of blood
and lie on my back in the truck

and think of the arms of my beloved
I didn't give away.

*

After the beating,
I could cut the dark with a knife,
if I had one.

I lie on the floor of the cell
and hear the shuffle of many feet moving,
slapping the cement.

I can't see, but I feel it.

I cover my mouth with the kerchief
so it won't slither inside me.

The lizard sniffs my breath,
knows I'm still alive

and leaves.

*

They beat me,
but I didn't breathe a word,

You can beat me
until the bones fall off my spine
and I won't tell you anything, I said,

I won't sell you my beloved
no matter what you do.

*

After the beating,
the guards go back to their room
to drink and play cards.

I'm glad I didn't whisper any name.

After the beating,
God lies next to me
and tells me *One more day.*

Valea Piersicilor
Romania, 1950s

Blindfolded, the students and their teacher
are taken to the Peach Trees Valley.

Their skin sucks in the bullets.

Chests jump,
muscles leap,

mouths open
as if telling something
to the fallen sun.

Scythed bodies,
limbs kick.

The dirt drinks
debris in a rain of blood.

Ion-Ioan-Laurian-Gheorghe-Jean-Victor:
souls caught in mushroom cups

and released at night,
when the owls laugh.

Oh green valley,
where the arms of the trees rise in surrender

and the roots kneel in the ground,
how quiet you are.

Oh deep valley,
where the peaches grow

fuzzy as the young men's cheeks,
how sleepy you are.

Oh, how sweet, how fresh
are your peaches of flesh.

My grandfather looks at the moon

The bleeding moon hangs
inside the clouds' ribcage:
a beating heart.

Up there, someone is still alive.

If only I could tug at his shirt
and say Look, look down,
look at what the merciless have done.

If only I could climb
on a ladder leaning against the night
and pull away the blindfold.

My Grandma's curse for the *Securitate* man

I don't wish you dead.
May you rot alive.

May you stink with a stench so strong
a thousand rains won't wash it away.

May your mouth be filled
with a hundred flies
for every word
in the reports you filed.

May your house and your heart
be torn apart
as you tore mine.

May you shrivel and brown
like a navel tied with string.

May your hair fall,
then your nails,
and your eyes be covered in boils.

May your flesh drop
from your bones
like the wax drips
from burning candles.

May the crows of the world come
in a black flood
to peck your eyes
and tear at your balls.

May your own mother dice
pieces of your liver
and throw them in the yard
to feed the chickens.

May you fry in lard
for the rest of your life
in the devils' pot,
with rats in your belly
and snakes in your cot.

For taking my man,
be damned!

For taking my sons,
may spears pierce your lungs!

May you get struck
by lightning and bad luck!

May you be hit
by punishment and spit.
May you nurse at illness' tit
as despair sucks me dry.

A Dirt Road Hangs from the Sky

May you roast in hell's pit!

May I see the day when you cry
tears of blood
as I cry today,
so help me dear God!

Mother goat and its three kids

Was my little son to your taste?
Was he fat enough?
                    Anna Akhmatova

Come, wolf, have a seat
at the funeral feast
held for the ones you ate.

Were my boys sweet?
I raised them sweet and polite.
Were their bones tender?
Were they afraid?

In my dream, I push you
into a hole in the ground.

I flick a match
and watch you squeal.

But I wake too soon.

You're still at the head of the table,

boots on,
stuffed with food,
licking your fingers.

My house is still empty
and I'll bring home today

> *no salt block*
> *upon my back,*
> *no corn meal*
> *in my high heels,*
> *no green leaves*
> *between my lips,*
> *no sweet milk*
> *in tits of silk*

and no grass, no hay, no hope,
only darkness's rope.

Where were you, house snake?

Romania, 1958

My sons were your milk brothers—
why didn't you protect them?

Where were you, faithful house snake,
when the beasts came at night
with sickle arms and hammer fists?

Where were you when the men in suits
came bearing guns?

My house is your house.
It keeps you warm in winter,
cool in summer.
It feeds you mice and milk.

You should have protected
these walls of mud and straw,
the one room where we slept,
the door the men broke.

I prayed you wouldn't let this happen.

I prayed you'd come and save us.
I prayed you'd throw fire from your mouth
and hiss to save my boys.

A Dirt Road Hangs from the Sky

Instead, you hid under the house's sole,
you gentle, coward spirit.

Tonight, the silence coils into itself
and bites its own tail,

but I can hear you in the wall.

Tick-tick-tick, you tell me,
this house is safe,
but the world isn't.

Tick-tick-tick,
the days will go on.

Tick-tick-tick, Maria,
learn to be silent
and slither underground.

Rain falls

Liquid bodies fall from the sky.
Rain falls like cut hair,
it falls with the sound of little feet
running on roofs,
soft as eyelashes hiding
the tears of a child asleep.
Rain tastes of tears, salty and warm;
rain falls with the taste of your lips.

Rain falls in a deluge for days.
There is no going forward,
nor back,

I send out the bird,
and it returns with a bone in its beak
instead of a green branch,
picked clean by drizzle teeth.

Rain falls,
and we walk through it for years,
through its bed sheets, dresses, and robes.
Rain falls, and we walk naked,
whipped by water ropes.

Rain falls,
it rains cats and dogs
and rainrats, and rainbats. Rain falls
with angel feathers and claws.

Rain falls, and the earth waits for it
with a thousand open mouths
until it gags on water and drowns
and the dust turns to mud,

the rain soaks the buried bodies
and washes them clean,
turns flesh into cold tea
we pour into cups and sip,

rain falls and seeps into walls
and into my clothes, day and night,
until my body pickles
in the brine of death. Rain falls

and the water fills every crevice and wrinkle,
it drives out the worms,
washes words
and memories away.

Rain falls.
It trickles and gurgles,
forms rivulets and streams that grow
into rivers that flood the plain.

Rain falls over the old and young,
it rains faces and hands
rising, reaching, grabbing,

rain falls and brings nothing
over me and you the same.

Rain falls. I used to like rain.

Something about me

On a moonless pond,
my paper heart sails

PART IV

The sky pours honey

The sky pours honey on earth
through throats of nightingales.

Dressed in black,
a woman scratches the earth's face:
sculpture of solitude.

Men and women with sun-baked skin
come from the fields,
lives ended.

The winged horse draws a carriage with hay.

A shadow on my mother's face:
we're leaving tomorrow.

The sun pours in water the white of fish,
the wind pours in the sky the white of herons,

the poplars pour in wind the white of seeds,
the sky pours in river the white cry of *lastuni.*

In this lake, once lived a catfish
that swallowed whole a five-year-old child.

Willows rustle, showing
their white, lacy undergarments.

The sun drives the clouds west:
herds of buffalos with sad human faces.

Here, an old woman slept in the reeds
with other winged and toothed creatures.

Villages rolled in wind, wind rolled in grasses,
fields rolled in forgetfulness.

At the gates, empty benches
for tired souls.

Crumbling churches,
walls deserted by the painted saints.

In the cemetery, the crosses turn east.

The road hangs from the sky
in poplar stitches.

People work on the edge of the earth;
some die standing,
others live kneeling.

Forgotten in the field,
their silhouettes write
eternity's gospel.

The sky pours honey on earth.

Hell is other people, Sartre said

In the middle of my life,
I wake in a shallow hell.

How could you, cousin?
How could you, friend?

The bread breaks in two
and bleeds in the middle.

You cut the corn stalks,
and I think of limbs.

You wring the clothes of the dead
and dress your children in them

and, every time you open your mouth,
a new reptile comes out.

Higher and higher,
you build your house

from bricks of lies,
of crimes.

After my husband and sons were sentenced to political prison: Grandma speaks

The house is an empty eggshell
from which someone has sucked
the amniotic white
and the yolk.

How will I breathe? I ask the wind,
and the wind tears the heart
out of my chest,
leaving a hole as big as Oltenia,
through which it whistles.

How will I sleep? I ask the night,
and the darkness opens
its toothless mouth
and shows me a place to curl
without being swallowed.

How will I carry on? I ask the snail,
and the snail shows me how
she packs the house on her back,
her sons' toys and books,
her husband's glasses,

and crawls on her belly
amid the shards of the village
for eight years, until,
one day, God finds her
a safe spot.

A Dirt Road Hangs from the Sky

How will I live? I ask the spider,
and the spider shows me how
she knots the night with the day
with the night and weaves
the worry with hope
into a home again.

The Eden Rose

1.
All night I listened to the thunder,
nectar of fear underarms.

Tobacco flowers and doors
opened and closed
with muffled cries.

Car wheels, soldiers, shouts,
Do you really have to do this?
luggage dragged on the gravel road,
mother's shuffled steps leaving the house.

Then, the ooze of silence in my ears.

The wind moved the leaves of sky

and, in the morning,
everyone I knew
was gone.

2.
Crabgrass crept in.

Naked,
down to the ground,
I watched the weeds' rise to power.

A Dirt Road Hangs from the Sky

I bloomed in secret,
releasing my scent only at night.

I cried rosehips,
pain ingrained in wood.

In spring, I grew hands
and climbed the trellis,
new thorns on my head.

I watched the road from the roof for years,
burning orange and pink

and waiting
for my family's return.

Woman of wind

I'll have to get used to living without you,
wearing the same dress of pain every day.

I'll get used to slipping my hands inside its sleeves,
carved not for arms, but for prayers.

I'll put my dress on without tears,
without thinking of you.

I'll wear the sky around my neck,
a scarf covering the scars.

I'll get used to my second skin of sorrow.
I'll get used to the hollow of my home

without walls, my living room of grass
and open space.

I'll get used to the dull days
and null nights.

I'll wash often my skin of sky
and wear it radiant,

empty, without birds,
or clouds,

or dreams,
just wind.

Why don't you come tonight?

Why don't you come to take me?
I asked death.

I left the door unlocked.

Bring your sharpest scythe,
or I can lend you a dull knife

to sharpen on
my heart's stone.

No, death said,
I won't come for you.

You'll be the one to bear
my many children,

the one to bake bread,
pick fruits, make wine,

and cook food for the souls
I already took.

You'll be the one to light the candles,
shield their glowing skulls,

and remember,
with cupped hands.

Grieving

My heart wears a black kerchief
and grieves

not for my man,
not for my sons,

but for this land of ours
that doesn't want us anymore.

Some men ran.
Some hid in the mountains
where they were outnumbered.
The others were taken at night.

Only the women are left
to tend the graves and listen
to the whistle of abandoned crops.

We can't tell anyone what happened,
because telling is knowing,
and knowing is dying.

But, someday,
my great-granddaughter will walk
on these fields stuffed with bones

where, instead of wheat,
the truth will grow from the ground.

When the dead come to visit

You knead the dough until numb,
divide it into small balls and stamp it,
leaving marks of the Holy Trinity
branded into the bread's flesh.

Thank God for flour, for hands,
for breath.

Kneel in front of the fire
and slide His body in,
until fragrant, with a crisp crust.

Fill the air with incense.
Pray. Pray.

Pair each pita with a lit candle
so the dead can see their way.

Next to it, balance a boiled egg,
a cube of sheep cheese,
red grapes.

You give me the food:
May it be for the souls of our dead.

Bogdaproste, I say,
and the bread changes hands.
May it be received.

From the scent of basil in her bosom,
you know your young mother Ioana
has entered the room,

and, when you hear the sound of water,
your drowned brother George has arrived.

The dead have come to eat, chat,
find out what's new.

They sit in the empty chairs around us,
share a bite of watermelon,

and watch me, a serious child
scrutinizing the frankincense smoke.

You tell them all about the garden
and how the kids have grown.

They ask if you're happy

and you're silent,
hands folded in your lap,

as you listen to the day drip,

this holy day
when the graves part
and the dead come to visit.

A song on the radio

> *Fall has come,*
> *cover my heart with something,*
> *with the shadow of a tree,*
> *or, better yet, with your shadow.*
>
> *—Nichita Stanescu,*
> *Autumn emotion*

A dirt road hangs from the sky
and waits for us to finish picking.

Fall has come.
We're picking its grapes
under the violet sky
soiled with violet juices.

A tremor is in the air.
Cover my shoulders
with your shadow
and a song playing on the radio.

Fall has come.
Our hearts are its naked grapes.

We crush them with our feet
and their dark juices sink
into the dark ground.

Fall has come.
It flows from the barrel.

Farewell is the young wine
you pour into the evening's glass.

It's sweet and tart like summer
with a hint of grass
broken under our bodies.

Take a sip, love.
Fall has come.

Love me

Green me,
watermelon me,
honeydew me,

of honey
and of dew
make me,

peel me,
slice me,
eat me,

and throw my rind
into the sky,
marked by your teeth,

and spit my seeds
over the rooftops:
brilliant stars.

Nothing here

There is nothing, nothing hidden in plain sight
behind the gray chair or in the clear blue pool.

And the rain didn't try to get to me yesterday
through the bus window,

and, today, the rose on the metal arch
doesn't say your name with its screeching voice.

There is no clue in the movement of wind
or in the warm flakes of light.

The cold water around my knees
isn't telling me anything with its slurred speech.

The heat of the sun falls evenly mute
on my skin and on weeds.

The trees point upward, but not to a secret path
only the birds can see.

There is no hidden meaning
in the way the ferns unfurl.

The drop of sweat clings and falls.
The fly flies.

You're not here.
There's no meaning at all.

Country road

Heady perfume
of flowering *catina*.

The sun, a blood drop
suspended on horizon's blade,

falls,
darkened,
on the crooked road

and is walked over
by cows.

The saint's rose

I went to the Maglavit Saint
to ask about you.

Instead of answers, he gave me
a wild rose
to keep in holy water.

If the rose dried,
I'd know you were in the desert.

If the rose made roots,
I'd know you were in the ground.

If the rose lost its petals,
I'd know your soul was free.

For eight years, I wove fields of wool
with roses that bloomed in bleeding nights

and they didn't dry,
didn't make roots,
didn't lose their petals.

All this time, I kept the saint's rose
on the windowsills of enemies and friends
and waited for news about you.

The day the rose's petals fell,
I knew you were coming home.

PART V

There is finally a bone in the heart
that does not break
—Marge Piercy

Don't tell anyone

Go to your room
and play there.

Don't listen to the grownups' talk.
And, most importantly,

don't tell anyone
what you hear at home.

Don't tell even your best friend
who shared her orange with you

that your father was jailed
when he was eighteen

for *conspiracy against the social order*
because of a poem found by the secret police

when they searched the house
for proof against grandpa

who said they could take the land
over his dead body.

Don't tell anyone
your grandma whispered in your ear

how she lost everything she had,
but her hands

that weaved against her will
red carpets for the ones who took all,

how she lost her house,
how she lost the land she had as a dowry

and the proud horses that could jump
over the eight-foot gates

but didn't.

The cane

No one was allowed to touch it.

The wooden cane was shiny and smooth,
glazed in lacquer,

with a steel tip and an arched handle
that spelled a perfect J.

It belonged to Taica, a short stern man
with blue eyes that wouldn't give anyone
an inch.

On Saturday nights,
he dressed in his best suit,
dark brown, white kerchief,
soft black hat.

He whistled to Schneider,
the German shepherd trained to heel
and attack,

and walked, swinging the cane,
chin up, on Main Street
to the village pub.

Taica ordered the dog to lie on the threshold.

No one could come in
or get out

until they pleaded for a while
and Taica had a few rounds.

He laughed, a raspy cough.

Late at night, when Grandma
didn't jump quickly enough
to serve him hot food,
the cane beat the dust
out of her back.

When not in use,
it sat in the corner behind the door.

The cane gave a faint glint
and watched me
like a dog waiting for my wrong move,

or the punishing scepter
of a king.

And he never did

My father stood in front of me, naked
in the hospital's basement.

He spoke to me,
his voice muffled by cotton.

There was water running down the green walls,
and a woman I knew in the corner,

face in hands,
sobbing.

Listen to me, Claudia,
listen to me.

I could see his lips moving,
but couldn't make out the words.

And all I could think of was to say
Cover yourself, Daddy.
You'll tell me all another time.

Still life with planks

We burn the bones of the evening
until only the smell is left.

My mother bends and lifts onto her back
pieces of an old fence she'll use as kindling,

and carries them uphill
until she disappears under trees,

where my father waits,
axe in hand,

to chop them into pieces small enough
to fit into the stove.

Against the wooden sky,
the broken planks,

a dismembered cross,
look almost human,

the stove's mouth
looks human,

the charred chimney,
human,

my parents—
petrified.

Dealul Robilor

1.
Without horses,
the prisoners pushed and pulled
the wagons loaded with corpses.

Dealul Robilor is pregnant with bones.
Plant a cross anywhere on this tomb.

Beneath our feet,
our fathers wait in the womb.

2.
The moon plays the pipe over the hill
as the men climb in single file.

Decades pass.

Who were they?
What did they fight for?

The kids grow without knowing.

Dressed as a guard,
the moon mows the forgotten names

and gathers them with a pitch fork
into haystacks.

Mother Goose

The village women call you
the wife of Goose,
your poor dead man.
You slobber me with kisses
I wipe off.
You point your crooked cane
at this and that,
at this one and the other,
as you did in your Communist youth
when you pointed your finger *You, you,*
and you, and you, and you.
You ate fear with the spoon.
Those marked were taken at night
and no one heard of them again.

And today, the sun splashes your hands
and mine with the same light.
Small talk spills like salt.
You sip the brown ring
from the bottom of the bourbon glass
and pose for a picture.
My daughter calls you *baba*
and hides behind my back
and you laugh, benevolent,
enormous,
your steel teeth intact.

The beauty of Fall

The body of an old woman,
my grandmother, taking a bath.

She unbraids her thin hair,
uncovers the skin unkissed by sun,

the unseen curves
of her arms and inner thighs.

The beauty of wilted flowers, of dry grass,
what is left of summer.

Facing death,
the dahlias undress.

My grandmother steps into the tin tub,
hot water ankle-high,

sliver of soap,
steaming vapor.

The grace of the maple seeds
taking their last flight through the air.

A rooster crows outside the door:
October's laughter.

I lather the nape of her bent neck,
rinse with a small bowl.

The sunflower bows its head
in acceptance.

A cricket sings
under the basil leaves.

What Grandma used to say when lightning struck

She says Saint Ilie is drunk again.

On a rampage,
he whips his horses that gallop through the clouds
and pull his carriage full of tin barrels.

Some fall,
banging loudly over our heads.

Grandma's crosses of air grow larger
as lightning draws nearer
and the village crouches
to the ground,
lights off,
breathless.

Her hands shake
when lightning strikes behind the barn.

Protect my enemies' children, God,
and my own, too,
wherever they are.

God, I'll kiss your cane;
lay it over the house, she says,

then the rain starts,
the good, clean rain.

Apple picking

Touch me,
lick the drop of sweat
gathered on my lip,

and listen to the sound
of this huge machine
that hums and churns,
and grows the apples round,
pumps the pears,
and turns beads into grapes.

Chir-chirr-chirrr—
an invisible assembly line
that swallows us whole,
hands and tongues and all.

The trees are charged with high-voltage juice.

Chir-chirr-chirrr—
root to stem to leaf to fruits and fingers,

the industrial sound of insect wings,
crickets' legs scratched,
cicadas thoraxes inflamed with song.

A Dirt Road Hangs from the Sky

Chir-chirr-chirrr—
touch me,
as wired blackbirds watch
and the grapevine swells
its thousand nipples.

Touch me,
but don't touch
the apples fallen to the ground,

or they'll throw you into the sky,
your hair full of flying sparks.

Where was I? you ask

You were a little seed
I carried embedded in my body,

so small,
like the kiwi seeds

in the fruit's bright green
translucent flesh.

At sunset, when I moved just so
against the low light,

the rays would shine through my belly
and I could almost see you there,

the pink hazy spider
hanging inside

by thin threads of tissue,
barely visible,

as the chick's seed could be seen
caught in a tangled cloud

when Grandma raised the egg
against the dim light of the gas lamp,

shaded the shell
with her cupped hand,

rotated it,
and squinted.

Photos in the pantry

Stiff strangers stare from their frames.

An old woman presides
over braided breads and cheeses in cloth.

Taica's mouth is stained by time.

Still, he looks so young
in his tight military jacket,
with his sepia-toned smile.

The door opens
and the great-grand-daughter he never met
bursts in,
her dress overflowing with melons and berries.

She reaches for an apple and bites.

I was her age when we twirled with dust
and loud radio tunes,

we turned and turned, and stomped
until the music stopped

and Taica panted *That's how, that's how
I'll dance at your wedding, my dear!*

The red string

I am bound to you with a thin red string
that runs from your belly to my navel
and into my daughter's body.

It's a thread of blood that trickles between us,
an invisible umbilical cord
that pulls us together like beads.

The string runs under my skirt
and sometimes I forget it's there.

I move farther away,
until the red wool unravels
and you tug at it in my sleep:

Come see me, you say.

It happened when my daughter was born,
a tender bead added to the necklace.

You spoke to me as I lay on the hospital bed,
aflutter with pain,
my body woven with wires and tubes.

The red thread pulled me through
delirious waters.

A Dirt Road Hangs from the Sky

I wasn't ready to let go.

I told you *Grandma, I'm not coming today*
to prune the roses in your garden,

but, everywhere I go, the red string follows,
dangling softly between my thighs,

telling me how close
is death's rose.

Turn your name to the wall

Send home the neighbors and strangers,
send them all.

Shoo the barn owl from the roof.
Send it to hoot the names of the dead
somewhere else.

Stuff with cotton the mouths
of the people in photos.

Stop their gossip.

Close the tired eyes of the Holy Virgin.
She has seen enough.

When evening comes,
stop the loud chewing
of furniture woodworms.

Stop the deafening ticking of the white snake
that still lives under the house.

Cover the window with a cloth
and a dark moth.

Turn the mirror to the wall.

Turn your face,
your tightly shut mouth
to the wall.

Let it be quiet.

No one will come through the door, only
the long candle flame.

All-Hallows-Eve

Trick or treat, says the doctor
to the dead man.

Trick or treat, says the scientist
to the lab mouse.

Trick or treat,
says the blade to the frog,

the wolf to the lamb,
the lamb to the grass,
the grass to the rocks.

Trick or treat, says the secret police
dressed in business suits.

Trick or treat, says the president
wearing a hero cape.

Trick or treat, says the old century
to the new one, dressed the same.

The Convoy of the Sacrificed

Inspired by the group of sculptures Cortegiul
Sacrificatilor *by Aurel Vlad, on display in the yard of former
Sighet political prison, Romania*

They bear witness.

They stand in rain or scorching heat,
naked, bald, huge arms raised
as if to shield their heads from blows,
or to surrender,
or implore.

They look old.
Eighteen men and women
in a group called a *lot:*
a large family—my father's?—
or close friends accused of conspiracy,
or strangers sentenced together.

They face the wall
that separates gray hell from hell

and none of them look to the sky,
to its cataclysms of clouds.

Some heads are bowed
as if they pray for us
or for their lives.

Some point in front of them
behind the wall,
to the future, us,
to me—

but nothing is there,
just bricks and mortar,
school children and tourists taking pictures.

Bones protrude,
bellies stuck to ribs,
empty holes for eyes,
mouths open with no tongues.

But they move their lips,
they speak, can you hear them?

They bring a message from the mass graves.

They come from history to testify,
to name the names,

carrying an era's weight of sand,
asking for nothing.

They teach us nothing.

No lesson here
about forgiveness or faith,
about survival,
loss or fear.

Blood dries on them like rain,
wounds close
until no trace is left,
no trace.

They march in silence
to the wall;

forgetfulness
kills them again.

To my native country

Country where I grew up in untouched rooms
with furniture covered in crochet,
windows covered with lace curtains,
and the past covered by silence,

Country that suffers from a disease
of truth dappled with lies,

Country where the former interrogators,
the political prison guards,
the ones who beat and spit,
the ones who judged and prosecuted,

who tortured,
who murdered,

are now retired grandpas strolling the parks,
enjoying their pensions,

one of them might even offer to push my daughter on the swing
while I run to the kiosk to get water,

Country where the ones who oppressed us for years
to advance their careers
now sign memoirs in the central library,

A Dirt Road Hangs from the Sky

Country in which some of the old still hope
to be saved by Americans,
and the young hurry to leave it all behind,

Country where the sparrows still chirp
about the Communist achievements,

the biggest one being the smashing of spines,

Country where justice is not only blind,
but also deaf and dumb,
and rides a donkey through the ditches,

Country where decades have passed
and no one was convicted,
no one found guilty,

while witnesses die,
addresses change,
the buried bodies dissolve,
mass graves disappear,

Country where it's no secret
the former secret police are disguised
as prosperous business men and politicians,

Country where the priests are still priests
after years of filing informants' reports,

Country of perpetual Halloween,

where I've seen my father cry
and the gravediggers laugh,

Wake up.

Shake off
these shameful chains

and show who
you really are.

The age of the innocent poem

The innocent poem grazes on the grass.
The air crinkles with light,

the cardinals hushed in the bushes,
and, under leaves, the ants hold their breath.

Clouds or mountains of unusual clarity
cut the sky with razor edges

and the cabbage thieves greet politely
the guards in the field.

I can almost hear the pea pods burst open,
whispering *Excuse me*,

and my young daughter didn't yet pull apart
the butterfly's wings.

Allow me another word,
Mrs. Grim Reaper Reality,

another sip from this warm brew,
not yet bitter,

another moment to listen to the lips
that rip the grass blades

and pull them into the poem's
soft mouth.

The dream

We meet again
at the edge of a black sea:
the tears you cried.

The water is as silent as amnesia.

Your dress is made of imploring hands.
Your hair howls.

When you speak,
the wind speaks,

and the grasses with a thousand mouths:

My memories are yours now,
these pearls of pain.

Take them,
give them to your daughter,
and tell her

Remember,
      we are
what we remember.

Verse

A man and a horse plow
the crusty field

dragging behind them
rags of dust.

The horse has a skeleton head
and still remembers

the soldiers' scent
and the interrogators' names.

Decades later,
the bones still talk in the ground.

At the edge of the earth,
the man and his horse bury

the sun's disk
and turn

to write another verse.

I write these poems for ghosts

I write for you, old women
who sit at the gates, spin yarn
and knit socks for the dead.

My every gesture is mirrored
by a thousand hands.

I carry these faces inside me,
on my back,
on my feet.

The ghosts don't let me sleep.

They gather on windowsills and roofs,
in the moon's breath,

and chat
with chattering teeth.

I write these poems for my father
who still hangs on in Skype,

to reach him,
fill the gap with words.

Hang on, Daddy,
hang on.

Here's a rope ladder.

Here are the words, Daddy.

Here's the blood,
the new heart,
the straw.

Men forget. Women forgive

Some men forget.
Some women forgive.

Each spring,
new grass sprouts

through the dirt
of the heart.

Acknowledgments

Grateful acknowledgment is made to the editors of the following journals, anthologies and presses where some of these poems first appeared, sometimes in earlier versions or with a different title:

5 a.m: The first 80,000 are hard. The next 2 million are easy
10x3: What Grandma used to say when lightning struck, Why Don't You Come Tonight
Alternating Current: The Dictionary
Ascent: When the dead come to visit
Big City Lit: The Moon, The Small Stone
Blood Orange Review: Where was I? you ask, The age of the innocent poem
Bluestem: The Gruel
Cider Press Review: Still life with planks
Connotation Press—An Online Artifact: Dealul Robilor, Don't tell anyone, For the forty soldiers of the XII Legion Fulminata, After my husband and sons were sentenced to political prison:
Grandma speaks
Cutthroat: Hell is other people, Sartre said, Valea Piersicilor, Mother Goat and its three kids,
Men forget. Women forgive, The things my father has seen
The Dirty Goat: My grandfather looks at the moon, The dream
Imagination & Place Press: Grieving

The Istanbul Review: One more day, Milk brothers,
The time when God lived in the river
The Houston Literary Review: A song on the radio,
Apple picking, Photos in the pantry
Main Street Rag: The cane
Oberon: Country road
Ocean Diamond: Verse
Poets and Artists: Mother Goose, The red string
Polluto: The blanket, The piece of glass
The Potomac Review: 1958
Protestpoems.org: To my native country
Ragazine: The Saint's Rose, Words Around My Neck,
The Convoy of the Sacrificed
The Red Wheelbarrow: My Grandma's curse for the
Securitate man, Where were you, house snake, Under
the table next to the door, Rain Falls
Respuestas—The Neruda Project: Love me
The Long Islander (Walt's Corner): The beauty of fall
Thethepoetry.com: I write these poems for ghosts
Wilderness House Literary Review: Nothing here,
Woman of wind

*

The Eden Rose was chosen as a Merit Award Winner
of the Franklin-Christoph 2010 Poetry Contest and
published on www.franklin-christoph.com.

Cutthroat nominated my poems for the 2012 Pushcart
Prize. Many thanks to Bill Root and Pamela Uschuk.

My father's friends in prison appeared as part of the chapbook *The System* (Cold Hub Press, 2012).

The first 80,000 are hard. The next 2 million are easy and *For the forty soldiers of the XII Legion Fulminata* also appeared in *The Rutherford Red Wheelbarrow Anthology (III)*.

Still Life with Planks and *Why Don't You Come Tonight* also appeared in *The Rutherford Red Wheelbarrow Anthology (IV)* and in *Wilderness House Literary Review*.

For the forty soldiers of the XII Legion Fulminata also appeared in *3 Quarks Daily*.

To my native country also appeared in *The Colorado Beetle (Gandacul de Colorado)*.

The sky pours honey appeared as a series of short poems in the chapbook *Ethernity's Orthography* (Finishing Line Press, 2007) and as a long poem in *Now Culture*.

Love me also appeared in *Touching: Poems of Love, Longing, and Desire* (Fearless Books, 2011) and in *Bigger than They Appear: Anthology of Very Short Poems* (Accents Publishing, 2011).

The poems *One more day, Dealul Robilor,* and *Valea Piersicilor* are inspired by interviews with victims of the Communist repression conducted by Lucia Hossu

Longin for *The Memorial of Suffering (Memorialul Durerii, Editura Humanitas, 2001)*. Many thanks for telling the truth, Doamna Lucia. I admire your work and courage.

The poem *The Dictionary—O* uses edited lists of victims found in the online archive http://www.procesulcomunismului.com/marturii/fonduri/ioanitoiu/dictionar_no/ and in *Dictionar N-O* (Editura Masina de scris, Bucharest, 2005). My gratitude and respect go to Cicerone Ionitoiu, Mihaela Andreiovici, Alex Stefanescu, and the group of Romanian writers and researchers who gathered, edited, and posted this information online.

Many thanks to my teacher Jim Klein and to The Red Wheelbarrow Poets for their constant support, friendship, and feedback. I am fortunate to be a part of your group.

Hats off to poet and friend George Held for reading and correcting this manuscript. Thanks so much for your encouragement and support.

*

To Ionut and Dana, va iubesc.

Notes & Bibliography

When justice can't serve as a form of memory, memory alone can serve as a form of justice.
Epigraph from Ana Blandiana's speech at the inauguration of the Sighet Memorial, also added as an inscription at the Sighet museum in 1993. (http://www.memorialsighet.ro/index. php?option=com_content&view=article&id=1051% 3A22-plus-nr-314-memorialul-sighet-la-majorat-memoria-ca-form-de-justiie&catid=39%3Arevista-presei&Itemid=91&lang=ro)

For the forty soldiers of the XII Legion Fulminata
Every year, on March 9th, Romanians celebrate The 40 Saints (Mucenici), commemorating the deaths of 40 Roman soldiers of the XII Legion Fulminata. They were Christian and were tortured for their beliefs and left to die on the banks of lake Sevasta, in present day Armenia. For the occasion, Romanian women bake a special cake called *macinici*, which has dough similar to panettone. The men might drink 40 glasses of wine, one for every saint. Over time, the celebration became a day of remembrance of all the unknown victims of violence, the John and Jane Does of the world.

The first 80,000 are hard. The next 2 million are easy
Gheorghe Gheorghiu-Dej, the first Romanian Communist president, bragged that 80,000 peasants were arrested for the crime of resisting the nationalization of the land between 1949 and 1951(http://www.revista22.ro/romulus-rusan-taranii-si-comunismul-o-expozitie-a-fundatiei-academia-c-5698.html). It's estimated that, by 1989, the total number of victims of the Romanian Communist regime reached 2 million.

The Dictionary—O
The poem uses edited lists of victims found in the online archive *Procesul Comunismului (The Trial of Communism)* http://www.procesulcomunismului. com/marturii/fonduri/ioanitoiu/dictionar_no/ and in *Dictionar N-O* by Cicerone Ionitoiu (Editura Masina de scris, Bucharest, 2005).

The lists of words are selections from *The Merriam-Webster Thesaurus,* Pocket Books, 1978.

The things my father has seen
Poem inspired by my father's stories from the Romanian Gulag. Leptospirosis is a rare and severe bacterial infection caused by exposure to the *Leptospira* bacteria, which can be found in fresh water that has been contaminated by animal urine. It occurs in warmer climates. If not treated promptly, its complications can be life threatening and may cause blindness.

My father's quiet friends in prison, 1958-1962
Series of poems inspired by my father's stories from the Romanian Gulag. He was sentenced in 1958 to 8 years from which he served 5 in various prisons (*Craiova, Gherla, Giurgiu*) and forced labor camps (*Salcia, Periprava*). He learned French and how to play chess in prison from other detainees. He was released in 1962.

One more day
This poem is dedicated to Elisabeta Rizea, 1912– October 6, 2003, a peasant woman who was tortured and sentenced to 25 years in prison because she helped the anti-Communist resistance in the Fagaras Mountains in the '50s. (*Memorialul Durerii*, Editura Humanitas, Bucharest, 2001, pg. 274-276). Her husband was among those to whom she gave shelter and food.

Valea Piersicilor
The Peach Trees Valley, execution site for the political detainees from the Jilava prison near Bucharest. Here, the last group of partisans, who resisted in the Fagaras Mountains to the forceful installation of the Communist regime, was executed in 1957. They were five students and their teacher (*Memorialul Durerii*, Editura Humanitas, Bucharest, 2001, pg. 79).

My Grandma's curse for the *Securitate* man
Securitate: the Romanian secret police, which served as the most active repression instrument in Communist Romania until 1989.

Mother goat and its three kids
Epigraph form Anna Akhmatova's *Imitation from the Armenian* (*Akhmatova Poems*, translated by D.M. Thomas, Alfred A. Knopf, 2006).

The poem is inspired by the Romanian tale *Mother goat and its three kids (Capra cu trei iezi)* written by Ion Creanga, in which a wolf eats two out of the three goat kids. In revenge, the goat sets the wolf on fire at the funeral feast. The poem paraphrases the goat's song to her kids.

Why don't you come tonight?
After Anna Akhmatova's *To Death* (*Akhmatova Poems*, translated by D.M. Thomas, Alfred A. Knopf, 2006).

PART V
Epigraph from Marge Piercy's *That Which Is Now Behind, Previous Condition: THE EIGHT OF SWORDS* (*To Be of Use*, Doubleday & Company, Inc., 1973).

A song on the radio

Epigraph and two lines from Nichita Stanescu's *Autumn Emotion (Emotie de toamna)*, published in *A Vision of Feelings (O viziune a sentimentelor*, Editura pentru Literatura, Bucharest, 1964). The song with the same title was written and played by Nicu Alifantis.

The saint's rose

The Maglavit Saint was a deaf-mute shepherd who was able to talk after having a vision of God in 1935. He reached fame before and during the WWII, when the village Maglavit became the site of holy pilgrimage. I was born in Maglavit and spent the summer vacations at my grandmother's house in the village Hunia, about 2 km North of Maglavit.

Dealul Robilor

The Slaves' Hill, mass grave of the former political prisoners from Aiud, Romania (*Memorialul Durerii*, Editura Humanitas, Bucharest, 2001, pg. 113-114).

The Convoy of the Sacrificed

After Margaret Atwood's *They give evidence* (*The Door*, Houghton Mifflin Company, 2007).

CLAUDIA SEREA is a Romanian-born poet who immigrated to the U.S. in 1995. Her poems and translations have appeared in *New Letters, 5 a.m., Meridian, Word Riot, Apple Valley Review, The Red Wheelbarrow,* and many others.

A two-time Pushcart Prize and Best of the Net nominee, she is the author of two other full-length poetry collections: *Angels & Beasts* (Phoenicia Publishing, Canada, 2012), and *To Part Is to Die a Little* (Cervená Barva Press, forthcoming). She also published the chapbooks *The System* (Cold Hub Press, New Zealand, 2012), *With the Strike of a Match* (White Knuckles Press, 2011), and *Eternity's Orthography* (Finishing Line Press, 2007).

Together with Paul Doru Mugur and Adam J. Sorkin, Serea co-edited and co-translated *The Vanishing Point That Whistles, an Anthology of Contemporary Romanian Poetry* (Talisman House Publishing, 2011). She also translated from the Romanian Adina Dabija's *Beautybeast* (NorthShore Press, 2012).

Claudia Serea belongs to the poetry group *The Red Wheelbarrow Poets* in Rutherford, New Jersey, and maintains their blog. She lives in New Jersey and works in New York. More at http://cserea.tumblr.com.

www.ingramcontent.com/pod-product-compliance
Lightning Source LLC
LaVergne TN
LVHW091224080426
835509LV00009B/1150